ISBN: 978-1-7333696-7-1

Front cover image by Kimberly M. Nesmith.
Book design by Kimberly M. Nesmith.

Printed by Ms. Education Consulting & Publishing, LLC, in the United States of America.

First printing edition 2023.

www.kimberlymnesmith.com

MANAGE THE MONEY, DON'T LET IT MANAGE YOU

MONTHLY FINANCIAL PLANNING

Introduction

Money! We can't live with it and we can't live without. In today's society, so many of us struggle with managing our money. Social media shows us so much that we want, but how much of it do we really need? We often say to ourselves, "Oh, that cute handbag isn't that much and I deserve it." And hours or days later, we're regretting that purchase or wondering, "Where did all my money go?"

With Manage the Money, Don't Let it Manage You, you'll be able to do just that...manage the money. No matter how much we make, we still need to know what's coming in and what's going out. With expense trackers, monthly budget planners, debt snowball trackers, subscription trackers, and so much more, you'll be able to manage your money.

Don't let money management stress you out. Take control of your money with this made for you budget tracker that will allow you to easily track your income and expenses, set financial goals and stay on top of your finances the way you've always wanted to.

How This Journal Works

1-DREAM BIG DREAMS

Everyone has big dreams-no matter how small they may seem to others. Dreams are great, but even better when they become reality. Write your financial dreams down and work to make them a reality.

2-BREAK THEM DOWN

Circle one or two of those dreams. Maybe it's save towards a new car, pay off credit card debt, or buy a new house. Now write all of the steps that will help you achieve those dreams. Then it's time for transfer.

3-PUT IN THE WORK

Now that you know how to get to those dreams in smaller, more attainable steps, transfer these steps to your monthly and weekly layouts to ensure you are making progress.

4-REFLECT

At the end of each month, schedule some time to sit down and reflect on your dreams, the goals you set for yourself, and the progress you made. Watch those dreams become a reality!

Dream Big Brain Dump

Use the space below to dump all of your dreams and aspirations from your brain to paper. Feel free to express your dreams in any way you'd like (pictures, words, lists, symbols, etc.).

Break Them Down

Now, it's time to break those big dreams into small attainable goals. Write all of the steps that will help you achieve your goals. Be as specific as possible.

DREAM 1

I will ______________________

____

____

Steps to achieve this goal:

____

____

____

____

____

____

____

____

____

____

____

____

____

____

____

____

____

____

DREAM 2

I will ______________________

____

____

Steps to achieve this goal:

____

____

____

____

____

____

____

____

____

____

____

____

____

____

____

____

____

____

PUT IN THE WORK

Now, it's time to put in the work. Schedule a time with yourself each week to prepare for the week. Start by thinking about your week. What you need to pay, purchase, or save for? Look at your income, and determine what your plan of action is. Set a focus for the week and determine how you will reach it. Then, track your expenses and watch how you manage your money!

REFLECT

You can't monitor your progress if you don't ever take the time to reflect on what you're doing. At the end of each month, schedule an appointment with yourself to reflect on the past month. How close are you to achieving those dreams? What steps worked to help you attain those goals? What could you do differently to reach your goals? What should you keep doing or what are you doing well?

MANAGE THE MONEY DON'T LET IT MANAGE YOU

YEARLY OVERVIEW

KIMBERLY M. NESMITH

TOP FINANCIAL GOALS

1

2

3

4

YEARLY OVERVIEW

YEAR_____________

STARTING BALANCE ______________________________

ENDING BALANCE ______________________________

Month	Income	Expenses	Savings	Debt	Giving
January					
February					
March					
April					
May					
June					
July					
August					
September					
October					
November					
December					
Total					

YEARLY REFLECTION

YEAR______________

What worked well

-
-
-
-
-
-
-

What I can do differently

-
-
-
-
-
-
-

Lessons I learned

-
-
-
-
-
-
-

My financial achievements

-
-
-
-
-
-
-

My motivators are...

Using the Monthly Planner

MONTHLY DASHBOARD

Each month, you have a monthly dashboard where you can plan out your month of finances-week by week, day by day. This way, you know when you'll need to pay a bill and look at your expenses in a monthly overview.

MONTHLY BUDGET

After your monthly dashboard, you'll see your monthly budget. These sheets are there to identify your expenses, track your income, determine your savings, debt, and sinking funds amounts

- Fixed Expenses are the expenses you pay every month like your mortgage, light bill, water, etc.
- Other Expenses may be items like your credit card bills that may change.
- Income is the amount of money you bring into your household monthly.
- Debt refers the amount owed to creditors.
- Sinking fund is a small monthly amount saved for a specific (usually larger) goal..

MONTHLY EXPENSES

Used to track monthly expenses.

MONTHLY REFLECTION

Take a moment to reflect on your month, how you did financially, and think about what you could do differently.

IT'S NOT ABOUT HAVING LOTS OF MONEY. IT'S KNOWING HOW TO MANAGE IT.

JANUARY FINANCIAL PLANNING

JANUARY DASHBOARD

YEAR______________

	SUN	MON	TUES	WEDS	THURS	FRI	SAT
WEEK 1							
WEEK 2							
WEEK 3							
WEEK 4							
WEEK 5							

JANUARY'S BUDGET

FIXED EXPENSES

Description	Budget	Actual	Paid

OTHER EXPENSES

Description	Budget	Actual	Paid

INCOME	AMOUNT
Subtotal	

SAVINGS

Description	Budget	Actual
Subtotal		

DEBT

Description	Budget	Actual
Subtotal		

SINKING FUNDS

Description	Budget	Actual
Subtotal		

JANUARY'S EXPENSES

Date	Description	Category	Amount

JANUARY'S EXPENSES

Date	Description	Category	Amount

JANUARY'S EXPENSES

Date	Description	Category	Amount

JANUARY'S REFLECTION

MONTHLY OVERVIEW

	Income	Expenses	Savings	Debt
Budget Amount				
Actual Amount				
Difference				

Highlights from this Month	Challenges from this Month
•	•
•	•
•	•
•	•
•	•
•	•
•	•

Start	Stop	Continue

"MONEY GROWS ON THE TREE OF PERSISTENCE."

JAPANESE PROVERB

FEBRUARY FINANCIAL PLANNING

FEBRUARY DASHBOARD

YEAR_____________

	SUN	MON	TUES	WEDS	THURS	FRI	SAT
WEEK 1							
WEEK 2							
WEEK 3							
WEEK 4							
WEEK 5							

FEBRUARY'S BUDGET

FIXED EXPENSES

Description	Budget	Actual	Paid

OTHER EXPENSES

Description	Budget	Actual	Paid

INCOME	AMOUNT
Subtotal	

SAVINGS

Description	Budget	Actual
Subtotal		

DEBT

Description	Budget	Actual
Subtotal		

SINKING FUNDS

Description	Budget	Actual
Subtotal		

FEBRUARY'S EXPENSES

Date	Description	Category	Amount

FEBRUARY'S EXPENSES

Date	Description	Category	Amount

FEBRUARY'S EXPENSES

Date	Description	Category	Amount

FEBRUARY'S REFLECTION

MONTHLY OVERVIEW

	Income	Expenses	Savings	Debt
Budget Amount				
Actual Amount				
Difference				

Highlights from this Month	Challenges from this Month
•	•
•	•
•	•
•	•
•	•
•	•
•	•

Start	Stop	Continue

"DON'T GO BROKE TRYING TO LOOK RICH."

MARCH FINANCIAL PLANNING

MARCH DASHBOARD YEAR______________

	SUN	MON	TUES	WEDS	THURS	FRI	SAT
WEEK 1							
WEEK 2							
WEEK 3							
WEEK 4							
WEEK 5							

MARCH'S BUDGET

FIXED EXPENSES

Description	Budget	Actual	Paid

OTHER EXPENSES

Description	Budget	Actual	Paid

INCOME	AMOUNT
Subtotal	

SAVINGS

Description	Budget	Actual
Subtotal		

DEBT

Description	Budget	Actual
Subtotal		

SINKING FUNDS

Description	Budget	Actual
Subtotal		

MARCH'S EXPENSES

Date	Description	Category	Amount

MARCH'S EXPENSES

Date	Description	Category	Amount

MARCH'S EXPENSES

Date	Description	Category	Amount

MARCH'S REFLECTION

MONTHLY OVERVIEW

	Income	Expenses	Savings	Debt
Budget Amount				
Actual Amount				
Difference				

Highlights from this Month	Challenges from this Month
•	•
•	•
•	•
•	•
•	•
•	•
•	•

Start	Stop	Continue

"REMEMBER THE GOAL AND NEVER GIVE UP."

APRIL FINANCIAL PLANNING

APRIL DASHBOARD

YEAR_______________

	SUN	MON	TUES	WEDS	THURS	FRI	SAT
WEEK 1							
WEEK 2							
WEEK 3							
WEEK 4							
WEEK 5							

APRIL'S BUDGET

FIXED EXPENSES

Description	Budget	Actual	Paid

OTHER EXPENSES

Description	Budget	Actual	Paid

INCOME	AMOUNT
Subtotal	

SAVINGS

Description	Budget	Actual
Subtotal		

DEBT

Description	Budget	Actual
Subtotal		

SINKING FUNDS

Description	Budget	Actual
Subtotal		

APRIL'S EXPENSES

Date	Description	Category	Amount

APRIL'S EXPENSES

Date	Description	Category	Amount

APRIL'S EXPENSES

Date	Description	Category	Amount

APRIL'S REFLECTION

MONTHLY OVERVIEW

	Income	Expenses	Savings	Debt
Budget Amount				
Actual Amount				
Difference				

Highlights from this Month	Challenges from this Month
•	•
•	•
•	•
•	•
•	•
•	•
•	•

Start	Stop	Continue

"MY MIND ON MY MONEY AND MY MONEY ON MY MIND."

ICE CUBE

MAY FINANCIAL PLANNING

MAY DASHBOARD

YEAR______________

	SUN	MON	TUES	WEDS	THURS	FRI	SAT
WEEK 1							
WEEK 2							
WEEK 3							
WEEK 4							
WEEK 5							

MAY'S BUDGET

FIXED EXPENSES

Description	Budget	Actual	Paid

OTHER EXPENSES

Description	Budget	Actual	Paid

INCOME	AMOUNT
Subtotal	

SAVINGS

Description	Budget	Actual
Subtotal		

DEBT

Description	Budget	Actual
Subtotal		

SINKING FUNDS

Description	Budget	Actual
Subtotal		

MAY'S EXPENSES

Date	Description	Category	Amount

MAY'S EXPENSES

Date	Description	Category	Amount

MAY'S EXPENSES

Date	Description	Category	Amount

MAY'S REFLECTION

MONTHLY OVERVIEW

	Income	Expenses	Savings	Debt
Budget Amount				
Actual Amount				
Difference				

Highlights from this Month	Challenges from this Month
•	•
•	•
•	•
•	•
•	•
•	•
•	•

Start	Stop	Continue

"IF IT AIN'T MAKING ME MONEY, MAKING ME BETTER OR MAKING ME HAPPY... AIN'T MAKING TIME FOR IT."

ANDRE' 3000

JUNE FINANCIAL PLANNING

JUNE DASHBOARD

YEAR______________

	SUN	MON	TUES	WEDS	THURS	FRI	SAT
WEEK 1							
WEEK 2							
WEEK 3							
WEEK 4							
WEEK 5							

JUNE'S BUDGET

FIXED EXPENSES

Description	Budget	Actual	Paid

OTHER EXPENSES

Description	Budget	Actual	Paid

INCOME	AMOUNT
Subtotal	

SAVINGS

Description	Budget	Actual
Subtotal		

DEBT

Description	Budget	Actual
Subtotal		

SINKING FUNDS

Description	Budget	Actual
Subtotal		

JUNE'S EXPENSES

Date	Description	Category	Amount

JUNE'S EXPENSES

Date	Description	Category	Amount

JUNE'S EXPENSES

Date	Description	Category	Amount

JUNE'S REFLECTION

MONTHLY OVERVIEW

	Income	Expenses	Savings	Debt
Budget Amount				
Actual Amount				
Difference				

Highlights from this Month	Challenges from this Month
•	•
•	•
•	•
•	•
•	•
•	•
•	•

Start	Stop	Continue

"EVERY FINANCIAL DECISION YOU MAKE SHOULD BE DRIVEN BY SOMETHING YOU VALUE."

JULY FINANCIAL PLANNING

JULY DASHBOARD

YEAR______________

	SUN	MON	TUES	WEDS	THURS	FRI	SAT
WEEK 1							
WEEK 2							
WEEK 3							
WEEK 4							
WEEK 5							

JULY'S BUDGET

FIXED EXPENSES

Description	Budget	Actual	Paid

OTHER EXPENSES

Description	Budget	Actual	Paid

INCOME	AMOUNT
Subtotal	

SAVINGS

Description	Budget	Actual
Subtotal		

DEBT

Description	Budget	Actual
Subtotal		

SINKING FUNDS

Description	Budget	Actual
Subtotal		

JULY'S EXPENSES

Date	Description	Category	Amount

JULY'S EXPENSES

Date	Description	Category	Amount

JULY'S EXPENSES

Date	Description	Category	Amount

JULY'S REFLECTION

MONTHLY OVERVIEW

	Income	Expenses	Savings	Debt
Budget Amount				
Actual Amount				
Difference				

Highlights from this Month	Challenges from this Month
•	•
•	•
•	•
•	•
•	•
•	•
•	•

Start	Stop	Continue

"THOSE WHO DON'T MANAGE THEIR MONEY WILL ALWAYS WORK FOR THOSE WHO DO."

DAVE RAMSEY

AUGUST FINANCIAL PLANNING

AUGUST DASHBOARD

YEAR_______________

	SUN	MON	TUES	WEDS	THURS	FRI	SAT
WEEK 1							
WEEK 2							
WEEK 3							
WEEK 4							
WEEK 5							

AUGUST'S BUDGET

FIXED EXPENSES

Description	Budget	Actual	Paid

OTHER EXPENSES

Description	Budget	Actual	Paid

INCOME	AMOUNT
Subtotal	

SAVINGS

Description	Budget	Actual
Subtotal		

DEBT

Description	Budget	Actual
Subtotal		

SINKING FUNDS

Description	Budget	Actual
Subtotal		

AUGUST'S EXPENSES

Date	Description	Category	Amount

AUGUST'S EXPENSES

Date	Description	Category	Amount

AUGUST'S EXPENSES

Date	Description	Category	Amount

AUGUST'S REFLECTION

MONTHLY OVERVIEW

	Income	Expenses	Savings	Debt
Budget Amount				
Actual Amount				
Difference				

Highlights from this Month	Challenges from this Month
•	•
•	•
•	•
•	•
•	•
•	•
•	•

Start	Stop	Continue

"BUDGETING HAS ONLY ONE RULE: DO NOT GO OVER BUDGET"

LESLIE TAYNE

SEPTEMBER FINANCIAL PLANNING

SEPTEMBER DASHBOARD

YEAR______________

	SUN	MON	TUES	WEDS	THURS	FRI	SAT
WEEK 1							
WEEK 2							
WEEK 3							
WEEK 4							
WEEK 5							

SEPTEMBER'S BUDGET

FIXED EXPENSES

Description	Budget	Actual	Paid

OTHER EXPENSES

Description	Budget	Actual	Paid

INCOME	AMOUNT
Subtotal	

SAVINGS

Description	Budget	Actual
Subtotal		

DEBT

Description	Budget	Actual
Subtotal		

SINKING FUNDS

Description	Budget	Actual
Subtotal		

SEPTEMBER'S EXPENSES

Date	Description	Category	Amount

SEPTEMBER'S EXPENSES

Date	Description	Category	Amount

SEPTEMBER'S EXPENSES

Date	Description	Category	Amount

SEPTEMBER'S REFLECTION

MONTHLY OVERVIEW

	Income	Expenses	Savings	Debt
Budget Amount				
Actual Amount				
Difference				

Highlights from this Month	Challenges from this Month
•	•
•	•
•	•
•	•
•	•
•	•
•	•

Start	Stop	Continue

"A BUDGET IS TELLING YOUR MONEY WHERE TO GO INSTEAD OF WONDERING WHERE IT WENT."

DAVE RAMSEY

OCTOBER FINANCIAL PLANNING

OCTOBER DASHBOARD

YEAR______________

	SUN	MON	TUES	WEDS	THURS	FRI	SAT
WEEK 1							
WEEK 2							
WEEK 3							
WEEK 4							
WEEK 5							

OCTOBER'S BUDGET

FIXED EXPENSES

Description	Budget	Actual	Paid

OTHER EXPENSES

Description	Budget	Actual	Paid

INCOME	AMOUNT
Subtotal	

SAVINGS

Description	Budget	Actual
Subtotal		

DEBT

Description	Budget	Actual
Subtotal		

SINKING FUNDS

Description	Budget	Actual
Subtotal		

OCTOBER'S EXPENSES

Date	Description	Category	Amount

OCTOBER'S EXPENSES

Date	Description	Category	Amount

OCTOBER'S EXPENSES

Date	Description	Category	Amount

OCTOBER'S REFLECTION

MONTHLY OVERVIEW

	Income	Expenses	Savings	Debt
Budget Amount				
Actual Amount				
Difference				

Highlights from this Month	Challenges from this Month
•	•
•	•
•	•
•	•
•	•
•	•
•	•

Start	Stop	Continue

"WHEN MONEY REALIZES IT'S IN GOOD HANDS, IT WANTS TO STAY AND MULTIPLY IN THOSE HANDS."

IDOWU KOYENIKAN

NOVEMBER FINANCIAL PLANNING

NOVEMBER DASHBOARD

YEAR_____________

	SUN	MON	TUES	WEDS	THURS	FRI	SAT
WEEK 1							
WEEK 2							
WEEK 3							
WEEK 4							
WEEK 5							

NOVEMBER'S BUDGET

FIXED EXPENSES

Description	Budget	Actual	Paid

OTHER EXPENSES

Description	Budget	Actual	Paid

INCOME	AMOUNT
Subtotal	

SAVINGS

Description	Budget	Actual
Subtotal		

DEBT

Description	Budget	Actual
Subtotal		

SINKING FUNDS

Description	Budget	Actual
Subtotal		

NOVEMBER'S EXPENSES

Date	Description	Category	Amount

NOVEMBER'S EXPENSES

Date	Description	Category	Amount

NOVEMBER'S EXPENSES

Date	Description	Category	Amount

NOVEMBER'S REFLECTION

MONTHLY OVERVIEW

	Income	Expenses	Savings	Debt
Budget Amount				
Actual Amount				
Difference				

Highlights from this Month	Challenges from this Month
•	•
•	•
•	•
•	•
•	•
•	•
•	•

Start	Stop	Continue

"BEWARE OF LITTLE EXPENSES; A LITTLE LEAK WILL SINK A GREAT SHIP."

BENJAMIN FRANKLIN

DECEMBER FINANCIAL PLANNING

DECEMBER DASHBOARD

YEAR_______________

	SUN	MON	TUES	WEDS	THURS	FRI	SAT
WEEK 1							
WEEK 2							
WEEK 3							
WEEK 4							
WEEK 5							

DECEMBER'S BUDGET

FIXED EXPENSES

Description	Budget	Actual	Paid

OTHER EXPENSES

Description	Budget	Actual	Paid

INCOME	AMOUNT
Subtotal	

SAVINGS

Description	Budget	Actual
Subtotal		

DEBT

Description	Budget	Actual
Subtotal		

SINKING FUNDS

Description	Budget	Actual
Subtotal		

DECEMBER'S EXPENSES

Date	Description	Category	Amount

DECEMBER'S EXPENSES

Date	Description	Category	Amount

DECEMBER'S EXPENSES

Date	Description	Category	Amount

DECEMBER'S REFLECTION

MONTHLY OVERVIEW

	Income	Expenses	Savings	Debt
Budget Amount				
Actual Amount				
Difference				

Highlights from this Month	Challenges from this Month
•	•
•	•
•	•
•	•
•	•
•	•
•	•

Start	Stop	Continue

"MONEY, LIKE EMOTIONS, IS SOMETHING YOU MUST CONTROL TO KEEP YOUR LIFE ON THE RIGHT TRACK."

NATASHA MUNSON

BUDGET TRACKERS

ACCOUNT INFORMATION TRACKER

Bank/Vendor Name		
Account #		Website
Card #	Exp. Date	Routing #
Username		Password

Bank/Vendor Name		
Account #		Website
Card #	Exp. Date	Routing #
Username		Password

Bank/Vendor Name		
Account #		Website
Card #	Exp. Date	Routing #
Username		Password

Bank/Vendor Name		
Account #		Website
Card #	Exp. Date	Routing #
Username		Password

ACCOUNT INFORMATION TRACKER

Bank/Vendor Name		
Account #		Website
Card #	Exp. Date	Routing #
Username		Password

Bank/Vendor Name		
Account #		Website
Card #	Exp. Date	Routing #
Username		Password

Bank/Vendor Name		
Account #		Website
Card #	Exp. Date	Routing #
Username		Password

Bank/Vendor Name		
Account #		Website
Card #	Exp. Date	Routing #
Username		Password

DEBT SNOWBALL TRACKER

YEAR______________

January	Amount Paid				
	New Balance				
February	Amount Paid				
	New Balance				
March	Amount Paid				
	New Balance				
April	Amount Paid				
	New Balance				
May	Amount Paid				
	New Balance				
June	Amount Paid				
	New Balance				

DEBT SNOWBALL TRACKER

YEAR_____________

July	Amount Paid	
	New Balance	
August	Amount Paid	
	New Balance	
September	Amount Paid	
	New Balance	
October	Amount Paid	
	New Balance	
November	Amount Paid	
	New Balance	
December	Amount Paid	
	New Balance	

DONATIONS TRACKER

Date	Description	Donated to	Amount

SUBSCRIPTIONS TRACKER

Subscription	Due Date	Monthly	Annual	Amount

SINKING FUNDS TRACKER

Fund:______________________________

Goal:______________________________

Date	Amount	Balance

Fund:______________________________

Goal:______________________________

Date	Amount	Balance

Fund:______________________________

Goal:______________________________

Date	Amount	Balance

Fund:______________________________

Goal:______________________________

Date	Amount	Balance

SINKING FUNDS TRACKER

Fund:______________________________

Goal:______________________________

Date	Amount	Balance

Fund:______________________________

Goal:______________________________

Date	Amount	Balance

Fund:______________________________

Goal:______________________________

Date	Amount	Balance

Fund:______________________________

Goal:______________________________

Date	Amount	Balance

MY SAVINGS JAR

$	/ /
$	/ /
$	/ /
$	/ /
$	/ /
$	/ /
$	/ /
$	/ /
$	/ /
$	/ /
START	/ /

MONTH:

MONTHLY SAVINGS TRACKER

DATE	DESCRIPTION	DEPOSIT	WITHDRAWAL	BALANCE

TOTAL	

SAVINGS TRACKER

SAVING FOR ....

START DATE ....

AMOUNT ....

GOAL DATE ....

HOUSE SAVINGS TRACKER

SAVING FOR

START DATE

AMOUNT

GOAL DATE

CAR SAVINGS TRACKER

SAVING FOR ....

START DATE ....

AMOUNT ....

GOAL DATE ....

VACATION SAVINGS TRACKER

SAVING FOR ....

START DATE ....

AMOUNT ....

GOAL DATE ....

HOLIDAY SAVINGS TRACKER

SAVING FOR ....

START DATE ....

AMOUNT ....

GOAL DATE ....

"BECOMING RICH IS HARD. STAYING BROKE IS HARD. CHOOSE YOUR HARD."

ERIC WORRE

CHALLENGES

NO SPEND CHALLENGE

1	2	3	4	5	6
7	8	9	10	11	12
13	14	15	16	17	18
19	20	21	22	23	24
25	26	27	28	29	30
31	YOU DID IT!				

NOTES

SAVINGS CHALLENGE

1	2	3	4	5	6
7	8	9	10	11	12
13	14	15	16	17	18
19	20	21	22	23	24
25	26	27	28	29	30
31	YOU DID IT!				

NOTES

Made in the USA
Las Vegas, NV
24 November 2024

12572336R00070